Who Was Juliette Gordon Low?

by Dana Meachen Rau

illustrated by Dede Putra

Penguin Workshop

For Allison—DMR

Dedicated to Scout girls around the world—DP

PENGUIN WORKSHOP
An Imprint of Penguin Random House LLC, New York

Text copyright © 2021 by Dana Meachen Rau.
Illustrations copyright © 2021 by Penguin Random House LLC. All rights reserved.
Published by Penguin Workshop, an imprint of Penguin Random House LLC, New York.
PENGUIN and PENGUIN WORKSHOP are trademarks of Penguin Books Ltd.
WHO HQ & Design is a registered trademark of Penguin Random House LLC.
Printed in the USA.

Visit us online at www.penguinrandomhouse.com.

Library of Congress Control Number: 2021008895

ISBN 9781101995563 (paperback)   10 9 8 7 6 5 4 3 2 1
ISBN 9780593382585 (library binding)   10 9 8 7 6 5 4 3 2 1

Contents

Who Was Juliette Gordon Low? 1

Daisy Grows 5

A Proper Lady 17

Marriage and Money 30

On Her Own 46

New Ideas 57

Bringing the Guides to Savannah 66

Busy Times as Scout President 76

A Worldwide Sisterhood 94

Timelines 104

Bibliography 106

Who Was Juliette Gordon Low?

On March 12, 1912, in Savannah, Georgia, Juliette Gordon Low waited for her guests to arrive. Juliette liked to throw parties. And she was very good at it! She often invited other wealthy friends over to her home for lively conversation and fun. But this day was different. She was in her fifties, but she was hosting a gathering of young girls. This gathering was the first official meeting of the Girl Guides in the United States.

When the seventeen girls arrived, Juliette explained to her guests how much fun they would have in Girl Guides. They would explore the outdoors, play sports, and go on adventures. They would find ways to help their communities. They would wear uniforms and earn badges, just like boys did in Boy Scouts.

At this time in history, girls were taught many ways to act like "proper" ladies. In school and at home, they learned how to be good wives, mothers, and homemakers. Juliette herself was a proper lady from a wealthy family. Her whole life, she had tried hard to follow the rules. But she was always curious and willing to try new things, even when people told her she shouldn't. Juliette wanted to change the definition of what

it meant to be a lady. She felt ladies could also be strong, independent, and help change the world. Most of all, they could have fun doing it!

That's what she wanted to teach these girls. Juliette's joyful, friendly, and kind personality won over everyone at the meeting. Together, they recited the Girl Guide Promise, officially signed up, and toasted with hot chocolate. Eighteen girls became scouts that day—but one

of them wasn't even there. Juliette had signed up her niece, Daisy "Doots" Gordon, at the top of the list. Juliette wanted Doots to go down in history as the first Girl Guide in America.

The organization she started in America soon changed its name to Girl Scouts. From that first meeting, over the past century, Girl Scouts has grown, with millions of members across the world.

Juliette Gordon Low blossomed into a brave and caring leader and devoted her life to helping other girls blossom into strong women, too.

CHAPTER 1
Daisy Grows

Juliette Gordon was born on October 31, 1860. Her parents, William and Nellie Gordon, were pleased at this new little arrival. Her older sister, Eleanor, was excited for a new playmate. Juliette was named after her mother's mother. To avoid confusion between the two Juliettes in the family, they called the new baby Daisy, which was a common nickname at the time. This nickname stayed with her for the rest of her life.

The family lived in a mansion owned by Mr. Gordon's mother in the beautiful city of Savannah, Georgia. Her parents were wealthy. William was a businessman who bought and sold cotton in the southern United States.

Nellie was a strong and friendly woman who liked to do as she pleased. She came from an important family in the northern United States. Her family was one of the first to settle in the city of Chicago, Illinois.

When Juliette was less than a year old, the American Civil War broke out between the Northern and Southern states. Her father left to become a Confederate (Southern) soldier.

Her mother's brothers were fighting for the North. Juliette often saw her mother looking sad, and she would only see her father when he came home for short visits.

Juliette spent her early childhood with her big sister, Eleanor. They played together on the violet-lined paths and climbed trees in the garden. Sometimes Juliette and Eleanor had to dress up and go for walks around the neighborhood, but Juliette would much rather be free to play!

The American Civil War (1861–1865)

Slavery was a system in the South that forced Black people to work without pay. Wealthy white enslavers depended on labor from enslaved people to run their plantations and treated them like property. They bought and sold them, and often beat them and separated family members from each other.

President Abraham Lincoln wanted to end

slavery in the United States. Most people in the Northern states agreed with him. But the Southern states did not. The South wanted to keep slavery and chose to separate from the rest of America. So a war began between the Union (the Northern states) and the Confederacy (the Southern states). At the end of the war, the Northern states had won, and slavery was abolished.

Juliette's little sister, Alice, was born in 1863. Then the Gordon household grew even fuller when Juliette's aunts moved in. Because the country was at war, the family had a hard time feeding everyone. Mrs. Gordon's family sent packages of food from Chicago, but that was still not enough. The young girls grew thin and sick. They had to take spoonfuls of sulfur medicine mixed with molasses, but they didn't mind, since it tasted sweet.

In December 1864, the Union army arrived in Savannah, led by General William Tecumseh Sherman. Juliette peeked out the curtains to watch as the troops marched down her street. The Gordons worried that the soldiers would invade their house. Then one day, General Sherman himself came to the door!

General Sherman at Juliette's home in Savannah

Luckily, the Gordons weren't in danger. General Sherman was friends with Juliette's mother's family in Chicago and had come to deliver letters. Union generals often came to visit the Gordons—and one even gave Juliette her first taste of candy! General Sherman urged Mrs. Gordon to bring her daughters north to keep them safe. While Juliette's father was still fighting as a Confederate soldier, Juliette's mother bravely packed up her children and made the long journey to Chicago by boat and train. When they arrived in Illinois, the young girls, especially Juliette, were sick and close to starving. The doctor delivered the news that Juliette might die. But by the spring, she was healthy again.

The Civil War ended in April 1865. The North had won, and the South rejoined the United States. The Gordons traveled back to Savannah in August. Juliette was so excited to be home, racing her sister Eleanor up and down the porch steps.

But Juliette was confused. She believed her father had been a brave Confederate soldier, but she had also met many nice Northerners. When someone told her the Confederacy was gone, five-year-old Juliette asked, "Where did it go?"

Juliette's father began to buy and sell cotton again. Like many other wealthy Southerners, the Gordons had enslaved people working on their land. When slavery had ended, the Gordons hired workers to take care of their home and paid them. Juliette's parents had more children—William, Mabel, and Arthur. The Gordons moved out of the grandmother's mansion and into their own house just down the street. Her cousins lived right next door. Now there were lots of children to play with! The children visited their grandmother's house for tea every afternoon. She taught them manners and how to act like proper wealthy boys and girls.

But Juliette didn't always act like a proper

little girl! Although she was small and thin for her age, Juliette was filled with energy, bravery, and a fearless attitude, just like her parents. That often got her into trouble. Once, she knocked over a lamp, and her bed caught on fire. Another time, she let her cousin braid a length of taffy into her hair, and they had to cut it off. She would bring home stray puppies and kittens. She had a dog named Bow-wow and a cat named Kittle. One night, she worried that her cow might be cold outside. So she sneaked out to the barn and wrapped her in some of the family's best blankets. The next morning, the fine linens were trampled,

muddy, and ruined. When she had an idea, it was hard to get her to change her mind. Her family called her Crazy Daisy, because they never knew what sort of outrageous stunt she would be up to next!

CHAPTER 2
A Proper Lady

Juliette spent her childhood summers with her sisters, brothers, and cousins in northern Georgia. Her aunt and uncle had a large old house on the Etowah River. Some summers, there could be up to twenty children staying at the house. This is where Juliette's curiosity and creativity bloomed.

The children played on the cliffs, climbed the trees, and swam in the river. They used the schoolhouse among the walnut trees to play "hotel." They created their own paper money, and then bought "rooms" in the hotel, peaches from the nearby orchard, or rides in carts pulled by the donkey or goats.

Juliette wrote scripts, designed costumes,

and starred in little plays. She charged the adults for tickets and sent the money to help the Native Americans she'd met when she lived in Chicago. She wrote articles and poems for her older cousin's newspaper. She painted paper dolls for her younger cousins.

But when she went back to Savannah, Juliette had to go to school. Until she was twelve years old, she attended school at Miss Lucille Blois's home on Hull Street. She enjoyed learning, but disliked spelling. She simply didn't think it was important. When someone pointed out a mistake, she said, "Well, it isn't my fault, it's because other people drag in such fancy words."

In 1874, when Juliette was in her early teens, her parents sent her to a boarding school, as most wealthy families did if they wanted their daughters to get an education. She joined her sister Eleanor at the Virginia Female Institute in Staunton, Virginia (now called the Stuart Hall

Virginia Female Institute in Staunton, Virginia

School). Next, she went to Edgehill, a school also in Virginia. Her friendliness and humor helped her make friends.

Juliette learned history, literature, science, and math. She always did well in creative subjects, like music and drawing. But she was still horrible at spelling—and would be all her life! Unlike boys who went to school to prepare for jobs, girls were taught the manners needed to grow into proper young women. There were so many rules for young girls to follow. Juliette would get frustrated. She once wrote, in a letter to her mother, "Mama, I can't keep all the rules, I'm too much like you."

Juliette was always on the lookout for ways to help others. Back home in Savannah, she founded her first organization, called Helpful Hands, when she was sixteen years old. She gathered her cousins and taught them how to sew so they could make clothing for poor people in the city. But there was a problem—she didn't know how to sew!

Etiquette

Good manners, also known as etiquette, were important to wealthy people in the mid- to late 1800s. Etiquette books taught girls how to dress, how to walk, and even how to eat soup properly! There were rules for when to speak, when to visit friends, and when one needed a chaperone. In the 1920s, Emily Post wrote a book about etiquette that became very popular. Social rules were strict well into the twentieth century. While rules of manners might not be as strict today, people still consider it rude to slurp your soup!

The clothes they made soon fell apart. Juliette's family teased her that the club should have been called *Helpless* Hands.

In the fall of 1878, when Juliette was seventeen, the Gordons sent her and Eleanor to New York City to Mesdemoiselles Charbonniers, a French school. They studied French history and literature and always spoke in French. The students were expected to be proper young ladies at all times. Juliette learned how to be a good hostess, wife, and mother. She was taught manners, dancing, and drama. She was taught how to enter a room, how to curtsy, and even how to sit. The young women took a walk each day on Madison Avenue, under the watchful eyes of adult chaperones. They were absolutely forbidden to talk to boys.

Even though the school had strict rules, Juliette still found ways to have fun. She and her friends hid in the bathroom for secret feasts when parents sent care packages. One time during the winter, a group of girls ran outside for a snowball fight. When they returned, they were forced to

stay inside for three days. But the punishment was worth it! Juliette, however, did have a special privilege that the other girls didn't. She was such a good artist that she was allowed to walk alone to a professional artist's studio to study oil painting.

Soon, Juliette was ready to "come out" into Savannah society. When a girl came out as a lady, she was old enough to start looking for a husband. Her family showed her off to the other wealthy

families of Savannah during dances and parties. Juliette was no longer the silly little girl who had braided taffy into her hair. Everyone could now see the proper lady she had become.

CHAPTER 3
Marriage and Money

Juliette enjoyed her life as a wealthy young lady of Savannah. She and her friends had picnics and parties, went to balls, played tennis, and rode horses. Everyone loved Juliette—she was fun to be around.

Juliette returned to Charbonniers in the fall of 1880, to continue her art lessons and enjoy all the activities that New York had to offer. Her younger sister Alice was now old enough to attend, too. But after only a few months, Alice caught scarlet fever and died. It was a very sad time for the Gordon family.

After almost a year of grieving with her family, Juliette started going out with friends and having fun again. She met lots of men who were interested in marrying her. One day she ran into a family friend, William Mackay Low. His family lived in England, but he had grown up in Savannah and was home for a visit. He was charming, tall and slim with blond hair and blue eyes.

William Mackay Low

His father was a millionaire. When Juliette met William, she said she fell "madly and unreasonably in love with him."

But Juliette's father didn't approve of William Low. He thought William was spoiled and spent too much time playing sports and going to parties instead of working. Juliette was sad when William left for Europe, so she wrote him lots of letters. He never wrote back.

After schooling, young wealthy women were often sent on a European tour. Juliette's older sister, Eleanor, had already gone, and Juliette wanted her turn. She convinced Mr. and Mrs. Gordon that her time had come. So they treated Juliette to a trip to Europe in the summer of 1882, and she would be chaperoned by family friends. She was excited to visit museums and see artwork she admired. She was also hoping to see William Low again. During her travels, she found out William's father, Andrew Low, had been keeping all her letters away from William! He wanted his son to marry someone from a family in Europe who was wealthier than the Gordons. Neither of their fathers approved of their relationship! Juliette hoped they would change their minds.

After she returned to Savannah, in 1885, Juliette had to take a break from her social activities. Her ear hurt badly enough that she decided to go to the doctor. She had read an article about using silver nitrate to treat ear pain. Her doctor wasn't sure at first, but Juliette insisted the doctor try it.

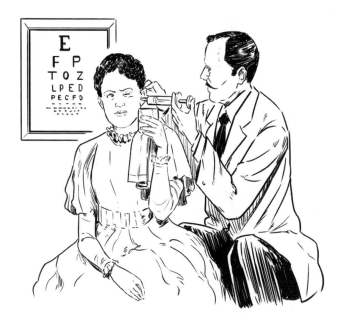

The doctor was right. The treatment didn't work. In fact, the pain grew worse. Juliette became ill and lost some of her hearing in that ear. During her illness, her father let William visit. The couple still had hopes that their parents would let them get married. William wrote a letter to Juliette's father to express his feelings: "Your daughter Juliette and I love one another dearly," the letter said. Mr. Gordon was finally convinced. Then Andrew Low, William's father, died suddenly. William was free to marry Juliette. He also inherited his father's fortune.

Juliette Gordon and William Low (or "Billow" as she called him) married on a sunny day in December 1886, when Juliette was twenty-six years old. Her bridesmaids wore pins in the shape of daisies. She carried lilies of the valley, her sister Alice's favorite flowers.

As Juliette and William left the wedding, the guests tossed rice at them, which is a wedding tradition. On their honeymoon, Juliette felt awful pain in her good ear. When they got back, the doctor found that a grain of the wedding rice had become stuck inside. The operaton to remove it caused even more damage. She lost all hearing in that ear. With only a little hearing in her other ear, she was now almost completely deaf.

After the honeymoon, Juliette and Willia
moved into the Low mansion in Savannah. It
was huge, taking up a whole city block! Juliette
liked to pat the lion sculptures that stood at the
entrance when she walked by. Even though she
now had to cope with the loss of her hearing,
Juliette was still excited to start her married life
with William. She brought the same high energy
she often had for any new project. She redecorated
the house with new wallpaper, rugs, and curtains
to transform William's childhood home into a
home of their own.

A Wedding Tradition

Throwing rice at the bride and groom after a wedding ceremony is a tradition that can be traced back to ancient times. Farming was an important part of daily life. The grains from different crops, such as wheat, oats, corn, and rice,

became symbols of good fortune. So to celebrate a new marriage, guests tossed grains over the new couple to shower them with wishes for growth and success in their lives together. Today, besides rice, people sometimes throw confetti, toss paper airplanes, and even blow bubbles.

By the next summer, Juliette and William headed across the Atlantic Ocean for Great Britain. They rented homes in England and Scotland until they purchased Wellesbourne House in the countryside of England. It became a huge estate with a full team of servants.

Wellesbourne House

Juliette and William spent time with other wealthy couples. Since they didn't need to work, they just found ways to have fun! They went horseback riding. They went to the opera and theater in the city. They hunted and fished in the countryside. They went from estate to estate, attending parties and balls.

Juliette always wore the latest fashions. She wore jewels that were gifts from William and dresses that dressmakers in Paris, France, made especially for her. She was invited to join an important family for a presentation at Buckingham Palace. She would meet Queen Victoria of England! She bought a special dress with a long train. Wearing all her diamonds and carrying a large bouquet of flowers, Juliette paraded for three hours with other visitors through the palace to reach the queen. In true "Crazy Daisy" style, she placed her flowers on the back of the dress of the woman in front of her when she grew tired of carrying them. By the time she reached the throne room, the queen had already left.

Juliette also loved having pets. She had cats and dogs, but she especially loved birds. Polly Poons was her parrot, and Blue Bird was her South American macaw. She also had a mockingbird that sat on her shoulder and snatched her pen when she tried to write letters.

Sometimes Juliette was homesick for Savannah. So she asked her mother and father to ship her some of her favorite foods. She threw parties with feasts of American southern treats. Her chef cooked up ham, sweet potatoes, pickles, and more. Every winter, she visited Savannah, and she invited family and friends from Savannah to visit her in Europe, offering to pay for their trips herself.

Juliette's friends enjoyed her entertaining personality. She was silly and funny and always had stories that made everyone laugh. There was a reason Juliette was so talkative at parties. Sometimes it was hard for her to hear conversations. If she misheard what someone said, she would laugh and change the subject. Sometimes she used an ear trumpet—

a funnel-shaped device used as a hearing aid. But most people she met didn't even know

Ear trumpet

she had trouble hearing because she was often at the center of conversations doing most of the talking.

CHAPTER 4
On Her Own

Juliette's life took a turn when she received some sad news from her doctor. Because she had hurt her back horseback riding, the doctor told her she shouldn't ride anymore. Juliette had to find other ways to keep herself busy when William and their friends went on riding and hunting trips. She turned to her art.

She carved a wooden mantelpiece for the fireplace at Wellesbourne. She painted pictures to hang on the walls. She also took classes from a blacksmith, made her own tools, and built iron gates for her estate. Her arms grew so muscular that she had trouble fitting into the tight sleeves of her Paris dresses!

Juliette also used this time to help the poor people living around Wellesbourne. She visited a woman in town who had such a horrible disease that no one ever went to see her. Juliette stopped by to read to her every week. She also visited workhouses to chat and laugh with the poor people there.

William did not approve of Juliette's kindness to the poor. He told her it wasn't ladylike. Juliette came to realize that William was not very nice. She did not like his spoiled and controlling attitude. When she hurt her back, William started to spend a lot more time away from her.

He took trips to faraway places like India, Africa, Albania, and Japan without inviting her along. In 1898, she took a trip to the United States to help her mother run a hospital for soldiers in Florida. She made them soup, tended their wounds,

and cheered them up. When she returned to William in England, she hoped things might be better between them. But they were worse. He had become mean to her. Sometimes he teased her cruelly by speaking softly so that she didn't know what he was saying. Juliette tried to hide the sadness she felt. But soon, Juliette wanted to find her own place to live, and everyone knew the couple was unhappy.

In 1905, William Low died. Juliette was on her own. Even though she and William had been married for almost nineteen years, he didn't leave her any of his fortune. But the courts decided that was unfair and made sure she inherited a large amount of his money.

Life seemed brighter. She was free from her cruel husband, had plenty of money, and owned the Low house in Savannah. Juliette wasn't interested in getting married again, so what could she do next?

Juliette decided to take herself on some adventures! She was told it was not proper for women to travel without male companions. But she liked to take on a challenge. In December 1907, when she was almost fifty years old, she headed off to India. The trip was filled with colorful marketplaces, beautiful temples, and elephant rides. She even dined with a princess.

She also visited Egypt, where she climbed the Great Pyramid. She loved surrounding herself with nieces, nephews, and the children of friends—many of whom she brought on her trips with her.

Pyramids in Giza, Egypt

Juliette also found more time for her art. She had already done so well at painting, woodworking, and blacksmithing. This time, she tried sculpture. In Paris, she took sculpture lessons, sometimes working on her projects for eight hours a day. She also devoted herself to helping others. Back in England, she volunteered

at a club for young working women in a poor village, and she discussed the importance of allowing working women the right to vote.

When she wasn't helping people or working on her art, she traveled between Savannah and Great Britain. She visited friends and went to the theater in the evenings. In Scotland, she rented herself a small lodge. When friends and family visited, she told them ghost stories about the fairy-tale castles nearby. In Savannah, she attended lots of parties, entertaining everyone with her bubbly personality.

Even into middle age, she still acted like "Crazy Daisy." Juliette liked to take her car out for drives—but she didn't always follow the rules! Her cook and butler had to stop traffic when she pulled out so she wouldn't hit anyone. Even then, she drove on the wrong side of the road! Once, she even drove into someone's dining room while the family was having lunch.

Juliette's deafness didn't slow her down, either. She kept up with the latest equipment and tried out some of the first electric hearing aids. However, she often relied on reading people's lips to figure out what they were saying.

Juliette had the freedom and money to do what she wanted. She was a lady—but on her own terms. She didn't need to be a wife and mother. She was independent. But she still wanted more out of her life. She wanted to make a difference in the world. Soon, a new idea would take all of her energy and attention.

Hearing Aids

In the 1800s, the main way for hearing-impaired people to hear better was with an ear trumpet—a large funnel-shaped device that they held up to their ears. In the early 1900s, new discoveries involving electricity helped inventors create some of the first electric hearing aids. People could wear these devices around their necks. But they were heavy, and the battery charge didn't last long.

Woman using a 1900s hearing aid

CHAPTER 5
New Ideas

Juliette with Robert Baden-Powell

In May 1911, Juliette met a man at a luncheon in London, England, and he would send her life in a new direction. His name was Robert Baden-Powell. Once he and Juliette started talking, they realized they had a lot in common.

Baden-Powell was a writer, outdoorsman, and artist. He was a curious and creative person like Juliette. She found him charming and caring, and they became close friends.

Baden-Powell told her how he had turned his love of the outdoors into an organization called the Boy Scouts in 1908. The scouts learned lots of useful skills like camping and wilderness survival.

Robert Baden-Powell with Boy Scouts

They also learned how to be fair, honest, and good citizens. Juliette wrote to her father about this new friend. "He is a genius as a soldier and he draws, paints and models as well," she wrote. "He left the army . . . to organize

Boy Scouts of America logo

the Boy Scouts and now he has forty thousand boys all over Great Britain, with branches in the U.S.A., France, and Germany."

Agnes Baden-Powell

Baden-Powell was impressed with Juliette, too. They met again at her home in Scotland. He told her that girls had also wanted to join the Boy Scouts. In fact, six thousand girls had signed up! His sister Agnes Baden-Powell had started a group called Girl Guides in 1910.

Robert Baden-Powell (1857–1941)

Robert Baden-Powell was born in London, England. His father died when he was only three, leaving his mother to raise many children by herself. When he was old enough, he joined the British Army. He specialized in scouting—gathering information about an area and the enemy to prepare the soldiers for battle.

Baden-Powell became a hero during the Second Boer War for defending the town of Mafeking in South Africa for more than two hundred days. He had written many military books  about scouting for the army and realized that many young boys were reading his books, too. So in 1908, he wrote a book called *Scouting for Boys*, full of his ideas about a new Boy Scout

Siege of Mafeking

organization. Many troops formed, and the Boy Scouts spread worldwide.

In 1937, Baden-Powell retired from scouting and moved to a cottage in Nyeri, Kenya, where he died four years later. His scouts had called him Chief Scout of the World.

An organization in which girls could learn new skills, become good citizens, and have fun sounded like a wonderful idea to Juliette. She worked with Agnes and started a Girl Guide patrol of her own in Scotland in the summer of 1911.

She wrote notes to the girls living in the countryside near her home and invited them to a Saturday afternoon tea. Seven girls came. One had even walked more than six miles to get there.

Over tea, scones, and cake, Juliette told them her plan. They met every Saturday over the summer, learning how to cook, how to administer first aid, how to read maps, and how to tie knots. Juliette also taught them the proper way to brush their teeth!

Many girls living in the Scottish countryside at this time had to leave home when they were young to work in factories in the city. It was

a hard life. A lot of them grew ill and died. Juliette wanted the girls to be able to find jobs closer to their homes. She had an idea—chicken farming! Juliette taught the Girl Guides how to raise chickens for eggs to sell to hunting lodges in the area. She also taught them how to spin wool into yarn. Juliette didn't know how to spin wool, but she learned from the postmistress (the woman in charge of the post office) in town, and then taught the girls. She found the girls a weaving shop in London where they could sell their yarn.

When the summer ended, Juliette left her patrol in the hands of the postmistress and headed to London, England. She wanted to give girls in the city a chance to have the Girl Guide experience, too. She started a patrol in a poor part of London. About twenty girls came. Juliette gave them not only hope for their futures, but the skills to take care of themselves, give back to their communities, and become leaders.

In January 1912, Juliette planned to return to Savannah. She needed to put her London patrol in the hands of another leader. She chose her friend Mrs. Kerr. Mrs. Kerr tried to say no, but Juliette ignored Mrs. Kerr's protests. Juliette said, "Then that is all settled." And she headed off to America.

CHAPTER 6
Bringing the Guides to Savannah

In January 1912, Juliette and Robert Baden-Powell left London on a ship bound for the United States. Baden-Powell was headed on a tour of Boy Scout organizations around the world. Juliette was going home to Savannah.

On the trip they discussed how she might bring Girl Guides to America. Juliette, as always, was full of big ideas, but she would need some help.

The night she arrived in Savannah, Juliette called her cousin Nina Pape. Nina was a principal at a girls' school. "Come right over," she said to Nina. "I've got something for the girls of Savannah, and all America, and all the world, and we're going to start it tonight!"

Nina Pape

Juliette told Nina about her experiences with Girl Guides. The girls would earn badges for each skill they mastered at home, outdoors, and in duty to their country. Girl Guides would be an official organization with uniforms, laws, and a pledge. Nina introduced Juliette to Walter

Hoxie, a naturalist who led an outdoor camp. Juliette asked her mother and her friends to be on the governing board.

Juliette with Walter Hoxie

Most importantly, Juliette reached out to the young girls of Savannah. She invited them over to her house and explained her plan. The first official meeting of Girl Guides was held on March 12, 1912. Eighteen girls signed up. She had enough girls to form two patrols that day: the White Rose Patrol and the Carnation Patrol.

Juliette turned the old stable behind her home into Girl Guide Headquarters. She purchased some wooded areas for camping, and she bought a boat for sailing on the river. Across the street,

Girl Guide Headquarters, Savannah, Georgia, 1912

she turned an empty lot into a basketball court. To play basketball, the girls wore pants for women called bloomers. Many people felt it was not proper to see a woman's legs. So the girls had to hang a curtain around the basketball court to hide themselves from people passing by!

Soon, more patrols sprang up around Savannah. Some only had six girls, while others had sixty! Juliette couldn't lead all the patrols herself. She found mothers or other women to volunteer as leaders. She handed them the British handbook written by Robert and Agnes Baden-Powell and said, "Here are the girls. You will start at once."

Amelia Bloomer (1818–1894)

Amelia Bloomer was part of the women's rights movement during a time when women were fighting for their right to be more involved in politics, to own property, and to vote. Bloomer started a newspaper for women, called *The Lily*, that she edited from 1849 to 1854. It discussed many of these ideas.

Bloomer heard of a new style of clothing for women—loose pants worn under a knee-length skirt. This idea was considered ridiculous. At the time, "proper" women wore tight corsets around their waists, long heavy skirts, and many layers of petticoats. But this clothing was uncomfortable and made it hard for women to move around.

Bloomer wrote about the new style of pants in her newspaper and started wearing them herself. Even though she didn't create them, pants for women became known as bloomers. They also became a symbol for women's rights in the late 1800s.

The girls sewed their uniforms themselves. They were blue with dark stockings and huge hair ribbons. The Savannah Girl Guides were able to show off their uniforms at the 1912 May Day festival at a Savannah park. After that, even more girls wanted to join!

That fall, Juliette's father died. She took some time to grieve with her family, but then went right back to planning and leading her new organization. The girls needed her. She wanted Girl Guides to continue to grow—not just in Savannah, but across the United States. She had a lot of work to do.

CHAPTER 7
Busy Times as Scout President

Juliette traveled often between Savannah and London to gather more ideas to help her Girl Guides grow. With tips from Agnes Baden-Powell, she made plans to take the Girl Guide organization across the United States. She talked to friends, family, and other women about gathering new members, finding eager leaders, and starting more patrols.

Munsey Building in Washington, DC

Girl Guides needed a larger headquarters than the stable in Juliette's backyard. In June 1913, she moved the national headquarters to the Munsey Building in Washington, DC.

The name Girl Guides changed to Girl Scouts, and patrols became known as troops. Instead of blue uniforms, which showed lots of dirt when the girls went camping and hiking, khaki (a type of brown often worn by soldiers) became the new color.

Juliette also felt that Girl Scouts needed their own handbook instead of relying on the British one. With the help of the naturalist Mr. Hoxie, she adapted an American version, called *How Girls Can Help Their Country*, released in 1913.

The handbook described the basics of being a Girl Scout. One had to be between the ages of ten and seventeen to join. A scout had to memorize the Girl Scout promise, law, and salute. The book described all the badges girls could earn. There were badges for sports and camping activities; art skills, like music and photography; science topics, like animals and astronomy; and household skills, such as sewing, gardening, and laundry. The handbook encouraged girls to think about future careers, too. They might decide to be homemakers, but they could also be firefighters, doctors, and scientists! The handbook also included the Girl Scout Law, which encouraged girls to always tell the truth, be loyal to each other and their country, and not be wasteful with money or time. They needed to be helpful, friendly, kind, polite, and cheerful.

Music badge, 1913

Naturalist badge, 1913

Designing Robots badge

Business Jumpstart badge

Girl Scouts Must Know

According to the handbook *How Girls Can Help Their Country*, Girl Scouts must know:

The Girl Scout Salute

- Three fingers up with the pinky finger held down by the thumb

The Girl Scout Promise

- To do my duty to God and to my country.
- To help other people at all times.
- To obey the laws of the Scouts.

The Girl Scout Motto

- Be prepared

Juliette traveled to cities around the United States to share the news about Girl Scouts. Some called her organization "Girl Scoots" because Juliette was always scooting off to her next destination. She always wore her uniform— a belted khaki jacket, white shirt, and black tie. She also wore her scout knife, whistle, and wide hat. Often, she would start up conversations,

and before the other person knew it, she had convinced them to join a committee or start a troop!

Her personality was like a magnet. Newspaper reporters rushed to get the story when Juliette came to town. Everyone wanted to hear what she had to say, because what she had to say was exciting news for girls.

At first Juliette funded Girl Scouts with her own money. She paid for all the travel, salaries, handbooks, uniforms, and more. But as the organization grew to major cities across the United States, she couldn't pay for it all. She even sold off her pearls in 1915 to keep it going another year. She had to start asking for donations from businesses, friends, and anyone who was willing to invest in Girl Scouts. Sometimes Juliette would bring out her "Crazy Daisy" personality to help get support.

Once, at a meeting, the discussion turned to

new shoes for the uniforms. To show the shoes to everyone, Juliette put them on and stood on her hands. Everyone gathered at the table could now see how they looked on her feet!

At the organization's first convention, in 1915, Juliette was named its president. The next year, the Girl Scout headquarters was moved to New York City. By then, there were seven thousand Girl Scouts, from all different backgrounds. Troops started in churches and synagogues. They started in orphanages. Troops formed in New York City's Chinatown, among Native Americans in New York State, and with Latinas in Texas. The first African American troop started in 1917. The first troop for physically disabled girls started that same year.

Troops, however, were segregated. That meant that white girls and girls of other races, especially Black girls, could not belong to the same troop. Racism—treating a group of people unfairly because of the color of their skin—did not end when slavery ended after the Civil War. It wasn't until the 1950s, when Girl Scout troops were officially desegregated, that girls of all groups could be scouts together.

Younger girls wanted to join, too. So in 1916, girls could join the Junior Girl Scouts (now called Brownies) as early as age seven.

Brownies, mid-1920s

As the organization grew nationwide, Juliette started *The Rally* in 1917. This monthly magazine, eventually called *The American Girl*, reported on the organization and its many members and was published until 1979.

In the beginning of 1917, Juliette took some time off to spend with her ill mother. Nellie Gordon, the strong, fearless woman whom Juliette admired, died in February. It was a sad time for Juliette. The whole country was about to enter a sad time, too. War had been raging in Europe since 1914. And now the United States had joined in the fighting.

World War I (1914–1918)

On June 28, 1914, an Austrian royal was killed, and this event led to many European countries battling against each other. Two groups—the Allies (mainly Russia, Great Britain, and France) and the Central Powers (mainly Austria-Hungary and Germany)—fought each other on many fronts. This global conflict would become known as World War I. The United States joined the Allies in 1917.

Soldiers and tanks fought on land while planes that were fitted with guns shot bullets and dropped bombs from the sky. The war was also fought at sea between the British Navy and German submarines. The war officially ended in 1919 with the countries calling for peace and signing the Treaty of Versailles.

Girl Scout national headquarters was flooded with messages from girls all over the country who wanted to become scouts. Juliette helped them find ways to help the war effort.

The girls got busy. The government had asked citizens to plant gardens (known as victory gardens) in their own backyards to feed their families. That way, all the food produced on larger farms could be sent overseas to the soldiers so they could stay strong and win the war.

So the scouts tended gardens and preserved the fruits and vegetables. They worked with the Red Cross, an organization that helps people in need, to sew bandages and knit socks for soldiers. They helped nurses in hospitals. The Mistletoe troop of Muskogee, Oklahoma, baked and sold cookies to raise money. This was the first Girl Scout cookie sale, which would later become an important part of Girl Scouting. The girls had found many ways to help their country.

Girl Scouts preserving fruits and vegetables during World War I

Cookies!

Most everyone has heard of Girl Scout cookies. After the Mistletoe troop's first cookie sale, in 1917, other troops started baking homemade cookies, putting them in bags, and selling them door-to-door. In the 1930s, commercial bakers started making the cookies and boxing them up for the scouts to sell. At first, the cookies were sugar cookies, but in the 1950s, scouts started selling chocolate mint cookies, too. Peanut butter was introduced in the 1960s. In the 2010s, Girl Scouts established National Girl Scout Cookie Weekend. Today, you don't even need to know a Girl Scout to buy cookies. Girl Scouts often set up booths outside supermarkets or other stores so everyone can buy a box!

CHAPTER 8
A Worldwide Sisterhood

After the war ended, nations began coming together in friendship. Juliette liked the idea that scouting could unite girls across the globe. She said, "Girl Scouting and Girl Guiding can be the magic thread which links the youth of the world together." In 1919, the first International Council of Girl Guides and Girl Scouts met in London. Juliette went as the representative of the United States.

In January 1920, when Girl Scouts of the United States of America had grown to seventy thousand members, Juliette stepped down as president. She was nearly sixty years old. She focused on growing the organization worldwide by traveling, giving speeches, and raising funds.

Girl Scouts in China, 1920s

Girl Scouting troops formed in China, Syria, and Mexico.

She also spent more time with the girls. When she wasn't traveling, she showed up at Girl Scout camps to hike, swim, and tell ghost stories around the fire. The campers called her "Miss Daisy" and even wrote a song to sing for her when she arrived:

Away down South in old Savannah,
First was raised the Girl Scout banner,
Daisy Low, Daisy Low, Daisy Low,
Founder dear!

Although she was often the center of attention, Juliette was keeping a secret. In 1923, she found out that she had cancer. She didn't tell many people because she didn't want them to worry. Instead, she kept herself busy with her international work for Girl Scouts.

Every two years, Girl Guides and Girl Scouts met at World Camps in England. In the spring of 1925, Juliette attended the planning meeting for the next World Camp. She wanted it to be held in the United States on land that Girl Scouts owned in New York State on the Hudson River. But that land was wooded, with no buildings or roads. Some people feared that they wouldn't be able to get the land ready in time for the next camp.

But Juliette didn't have much time. Her cancer was getting worse. She pulled aside her friend Jane Rippin, the national director of Girl Scouts, and told her the secret. The committee then decided that World Camp would be held in the United States.

Crews got to work! They cleared trees, made roads, dug wells, and installed pipes. They built cabins and set up tents. The workers were still putting on finishing touches when Girl Scout World Camp opened in May 1926.

Four hundred and fifty-six scouts (four hundred from the United States, fifty-six from other countries) attended World Camp in New York State. A parade of cars brought the girls up the road, which was lined with their countries' flags, to the Great Hall. Juliette greeted each of the girls. Girls came from India, Egypt, China,

Italy, Norway, Uruguay, Portugal, and many more countries. Even though Juliette was ill, she didn't let it show.

Juliette spent the fall of 1926 in England visiting friends. She was feeling so sick that she returned to Savannah in early January. She couldn't hide her secret any longer. Messages of love and bouquets of flowers poured in. When she received so many flowers, she said, "There won't be any left for the funeral if this keeps up!"

On January 17, 1927, Juliette Gordon Low died at her home in Savannah. She was sixty-six years old. At her funeral, Girl Scouts lined the steps of Christ Church. She was buried in her Girl Scout uniform. Tucked in her pocket was a telegram from the national officers of Girl Scouts, sent only a few days before. It read: "You are not only the first Girl Scout, but the best Girl Scout of them all."

Since Juliette's death, Girl Scouting has continued to grow. When she died, there were 168,000 Girl Scouts in the United States. In 2012, Girl Scouts of the United States of America's one hundredth anniversary, there were 3.2 million worldwide! Former scouts have included women in politics and entertainment, anchorwomen, judges, and astronauts. Tennis player Venus Williams and astronaut Sally Ride were both Girl Scouts. Michelle Obama was made the Honorary President of the Girl Scouts when she was First Lady. Juliette herself has been honored on stamps.

Venus Williams and First Lady Michelle Obama

She has had schools and ships named after her, and received the Presidential Medal of Freedom, the highest honor a president can give to a civilian, in 2012. Girl Scouts still salute and recite the Girl Scout Promise. Every day, Girl Scouts learn new skills, earn badges, and help their communities, just as they did when the organization began.

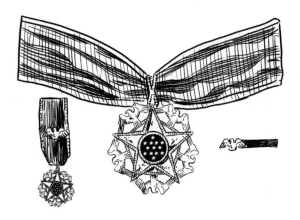

Presidential Medal of Freedom

Juliette changed the lives of millions of girls. She showed them that they can be courageous and kind. She showed them how important it is to be responsible, respectful, honest, and strong.

She encouraged girls to take risks and lead others. She proved that all sorts of girls, no matter who they are, can be sisters who work together for good. She believed that every girl has the power to make the world a better place.

Timeline of Juliette Gordon Low's Life

1860 — Born on October 31 in Savannah, Georgia

1865 — Flees to Chicago with her mother and siblings during the American Civil War

1878 — Starts attending Mesdemoiselles Charbonniers school in New York City

1885 — Suffers ear pain that leads to partial deafness in one ear

1886 — Marries William Low on December 21

— Becomes deaf in the other ear after an infection

1898 — Helps her mother care for soldiers in Florida during the Spanish-American War

1905 — Husband, William Low, dies

1911 — Becomes friends with Robert Baden-Powell, the founder of the Boy Scouts, and his sister Agnes Baden-Powell, the leader of Girl Guides

— Starts up her own Girl Guide patrols in Scotland and England

1912 — Holds the first official Girl Guides meeting in Savannah on March 12

1915 — Elected president of Girl Scouts

1920 — Steps down as president and becomes founder

1927 — Dies on January 17, in Savannah, Georgia

Timeline of the World

1861 — The American Civil War begins

1869 — The transcontinental railroad, the first route by train across the entire United States, is completed

1891 — Basketball is invented by James Naismith in Springfield, Massachusetts

1894 — Coca-Cola is first sold in bottles

1898 — Miller Reese Hutchison invents the Akouphone, the first electric hearing aid

1906 — An earthquake and fire destroy most of San Francisco, California

1911 — Norwegian explorer Roald Amundsen and his team arrive at the South Pole

1912 — The *Titanic*, a luxury ship, sinks after colliding with an iceberg

1914 — The Panama Canal opens, connecting the Atlantic and Pacific Oceans

1920 — The Nineteenth Amendment to the US Constitution grants women the right to vote

1921 — Spanish artist Pablo Picasso paints his famous cubist work *Three Musicians*

1927 — The Cyclone wooden roller coaster opens in Brooklyn, New York

Bibliography

*Books for young readers

Cordery, Stacy A. *Juliette Gordon Low: The Remarkable Founder of the Girl Scouts.* New York: Penguin Books, 2012.

Denny Shultz, Gladys, and Daisy Gordon Lawrence. *Lady from Savannah: The Life of Juliette Low.* Philadelphia: J. B. Lippincott, 1958.

Girl Scouts University, Juliette Gordon Low Birthplace, Girl Scout National Historic Preservation Center & GSUSA Interactive Marketing. *The Story of Juliette Gordon Low.* Girl Scouts University, 2013. iBooks.

Girl Scouts USA. *Golden Eaglet: The Story of a Girl Scout.* Filmed in 1918 in Central Valley, NY. Video, 19:32. https://vimeo.com/165428508.

Hyde Choate, Anne, and Helen Ferris, eds. *Juliette Low and the Girl Scouts: The Story of an American Woman, 1860–1927.* New York: Girl Scouts Incorporated, 1928.

"Juliette Gordon Low." **Georgia Historical Society.** http://
georgiahistory.com/education-outreach/online-exhibits/
featured-historical-figures/juliette-gordon-low/.

*Low, Juliette. *How Girls Can Help Their Country.* New York: Girl
Scout National Headquarters, 1917.

Sims, Anastatia. "Juliette Gordon Low (1860–1927)." *New Georgia
Encyclopedia.* Last modified October 5, 2019. http://www.
georgiaencyclopedia.org/articles/history-archaeology/
juliette-gordon-low-1860-1927.

*Wadsworth, Ginger. *First Girl Scout: The Life of Juliette Gordon
Low.* New York: Clarion Books, 2012.

Websites

www.girlscouts.org

www.juliettegordonlowbirthplace.org